UNITED NATIONS
KEEPING THE PEACE

SEAN CONNOLLY

Heinemann
LIBRARY

www.heinemann.co.uk
Visit our website to find out more information about **Heinemann Library** books.

To order:
 Phone 44 (0) 1865 888066
 Send a fax to 44 (0) 1865 314091
Visit the Heinemann Bookshop at www.heinemann.co.uk to browse our catalogue and order online.

First published in Great Britain by Heinemann Library, Halley Court, Jordan Hill, Oxford OX2 8EJ, a division of Reed Educational and Professional Publishing Ltd.
Heinemann is a registered trademark of Reed Educational and Professional Publishing Ltd.

OXFORD MELBOURNE AUCKLAND JOHANNESBURG BLANTYRE GABORONE IBADAN PORTSMOUTH (NH) USA CHICAGO

Designed by AMR
Illustrated by Chartwell Illustrators
Originated by Dot Gradations
Printed by South China Printers

05 04 03 02 01
10 9 8 7 6 5 4 3 2 1
ISBN 0 431 11864 7

British Library Cataloguing in Publication Data

Connolly, Sean
United Nations: keeping the peace. – (Troubled world)
1. United Nations – Peacekeeping forces – Juvenile literature
I. Title
341.5'23

Acknowledgements
The publishers would like to thank the following for permission to reproduce photographs:
Pg.4 Popperfoto/Reuters; Pg.6 Hulton Getty; Pg.9 Hulton Deutsch; Pg.10 Hulton Getty; Pg.11 Hulton Getty; Pg.12 Hulton Getty; Pg.13 Popperfoto; Pg.15 Hulton Getty; Pg.16 Popperfoto; Pg.19 Hulton Getty; Pg.20 Hulton Getty; Pg.22 Topham Picturepoint; Pg.23 Popperfoto/Reuters; Pg.25 Frank Spooner/Gamma Presse; Pg.27 Hulton Getty; Pg.28 Hulton Getty; Pg.31 Hulton Deutsch; Pg.32 Hulton Getty; Pg.33 Popperfoto; Pg.34 Rex Features: Pg.36 Frank Spooner/Gamma Presse; Pg.37 Rex Features; Pg.39 Rex Features/Sipa Press; Pg.40 Popperfoto; Pg.41 Rex Features/Sipa Press; Pg.43 Rex Features/Sipa Press; Pg.44 Popperfoto; Pg.45 Frank Spooner/Gamma Presse; Pg.46 United Nations; Pg.48 David King Collection; Pg.49 Frank Spooner/Gamma Presse; Pg.51 AFP/Mike Nelson; Pg.52 Popperfoto; Pg.54 Popperfoto/Reuters; Pg.55 Frank Spooner/Gamma Presse; Pg.56 Corbis.

Cover photograph reproduced with permission of Frank Spooner.

Every effort has been made to contact copyright holders of any material reproduced in this book. Any omissions will be rectified in subsequent printings if notice is given to the publishers.

Contents

Words that appear in the text in bold, **like this**, are explained in the glossary.

What is the UN?

The United Nations (UN) is an international organization of **nation-states** which deals with a wide range of international issues. An underlying principle of the UN is the **sovereign** equality of its members. The UN **charter** states that it was established 'to maintain international peace and security'; 'to develop friendly relations among nations'; and 'to achieve international co-operation in solving ... economic, social, cultural, or humanitarian [problems]' and in 'encouraging respect for human rights and for fundamental freedoms'. Countries applying to be members of the UN must pledge to be 'peace-loving'. As of May 2000, the UN had 185 members.

UN Secretary-General Kofi Annan holds the world's six billionth person, 1999.

The UN framework
The UN comprises six principal bodies: the General Assembly, the Security Council, the Economic and Social Council, the Trusteeship Council, the International Court of Justice and the Secretariat.

The General Assembly is its main **deliberative** body, and all member states are represented in it. In this respect it resembles a national **legislative** body, such as the UK's Parliament or the US Congress. The General Assembly meets annually in regular sessions and in special sessions at the request of a majority of its members or of the Security Council. The assembly has no enforcement authority; its resolutions are recommendations that carry the weight of majority opinion but cannot be enforced. The General Assembly also approves the overall UN budget.

The Security Council is the UN's central body for maintaining peace. It has fifteen members; five of these – China, France, Russia, the UK and the United States – have permanent seats. Non-permanent members serve two-year terms, with five new members elected by the General Assembly every year. Decisions of the council require nine votes; however, any one of the five permanent members can **veto** a major issue. In its role of maintaining peace, the Security Council may appoint representatives or set up special committees to investigate disputes and recommend means of settlement. If it concludes that a dispute threatens peace it can enforce its recommendations, either by non-military means, such as economic or diplomatic **sanctions**, or by the use of military force. These are the discussions and recommendations that lie behind the entire UN Peacekeeping operation. No matter how seemingly straightforward an operation, the Security Council must provide it with a clear **mandate**. The strict neutrality of UN personnel – either military or civilian – in any conflict is a distinct advantage, but the operation can only succeed if it has a clear focus and achievable aims.

The Secretariat carries out the administrative tasks of the UN. It is headed by the Secretary-General, who is appointed by the General Assembly on the recommendation of the Security Council. The Secretary-General acts as the UN spokesperson and can present conflicts that threaten peace to the Security Council.

The Economic and Social Council (ECOSOC) co-ordinates the economic and social activities of the UN. ECOSOC studies and recommends action on international issues such as health, education, economics and social needs. Although the Trusteeship Council still exists it is currently inactive. The International Court of Justice, situated in The Hague, the Netherlands, is the **judicial** body of the UN.

Leadership

Since the founding of the UN, seven Secretaries-General have held office: Trygve Lie (Norway), 1946–1953; Dag Hammarskjöld (Sweden), 1953–1961; U Thant (Burma), 1961–1971; Kurt Waldheim (Austria), 1972–1981; Javier Pérez de Cuéllar (Peru), 1982–1991; Boutros Boutros-Ghali (Egypt), 1992–1997; and Kofi Annan (Ghana), 1997–.

Modern warfare

The roots of modern warfare, with its capacity to kill thousands or even millions of people, lie in the 19th century. Before that time, conflicts between nations were far more localized, with relatively small armies pitted against each other in a series of decisive battles that eventually tipped the balance one way or the other.

The scale of warfare increased dramatically after the French Revolution of 1789. France, in an effort to protect its new government, mobilized huge armies by using large scale **conscription** for the first time. It was with these armies that Napoleon Bonaparte embarked on his famous wars of conquest across Europe.

German soldiers, part of a large European force, arrive in Beijing in 1901 to impose a political settlement in China.

Alliances and armaments

Napoleon's success, which put large areas of Europe under French control, sent shockwaves through the rest of the continent. Great Britain, Prussia, Russia, Austria and Sweden formed a series of **coalitions** to present a united front against Napoleon. It was the Fifth Coalition that finally achieved its aim by defeating Napoleon's forces on 18 June 1815 at the Battle of Waterloo.

This notion of shared national interests, tied in with alliances of different nations, would influence later thinking about how to conduct war – and how to maintain peace. Out of this thinking arose the Triple Alliance of 1882, involving Germany, Austria-Hungary and Italy. This development alarmed France, Great Britain and Russia, who concluded a rival alliance known as the Triple **Entente**. The end of the 19th century was a time of peace, but there was an underlying – and growing – sense of tension caused by the rival alliances.

The inevitable explosion

By the beginning of the 20th century the tension between Europe's main military powers became acute. Many of them had acquired foreign empires and the European rivalries were played out in Asia and Africa. Attitudes hardened, threats became common and finally, in August 1914, war broke out in Europe. Men eagerly enlisted to fight in what was called the Great War, but which has since become known as the First World War.

It was during this war that the system of alliances came back to haunt Europe. The balance of power, which had been so painstakingly preserved in the 19th century, still seemed to hold. Neither side could establish its hoped-for early advantage, and the war dragged on for more than four years. The gallant cavalry charges and stirring calls to arms – part of European warfare for centuries – were replaced by monotonous trench warfare, aerial bombing and poison gas attacks. Eventually, some 32 countries were involved in the fighting, including the United States, which entered in 1917. The war saw some of the worst bloodshed in history: 8.5 million troops were killed and another 29 million were wounded or missing. In addition, nearly 10 million civilians died as a result of the fighting.

Revolutionary fears

The turbulent years of the First World War saw another incident of profound importance – the Russian Revolution. For centuries Russia was ruled by tsars, whose governments were largely undemocratic and **repressive**. Conditions for the poorest workers and peasants were difficult and any demonstration in favour of reform was crushed. In March 1917, with the government and army concentrating on fighting the war, a popular revolution overthrew Tsar Nicholas II and set up a new government. This moderate government was in turn overthrown eight months later by hard-line **communists** known as Bolsheviks.

Russia's new revolutionary government quickly negotiated an end to Russia's involvement in the war, but almost immediately began calling for other nations to throw down their arms. In essence, Russia was calling for the workers of other countries to set up similar communist governments – although the language was mainly concerned with peace. Despite the ferocity of the fighting in the war, nearly every other country was terrified by the possible spread of communism. This fear continued after the war and many people now see Wilson's plans for a League of Nations as a response to the communist peace offer.

The League of Nations

The world was appalled by the effects of the First World War. US President Woodrow Wilson, who helped draw up the Treaty of Versailles ending the First World War, proposed a plan for a general association of nations. It formed the basis of the League of Nations, which met for the first time on 15 November 1920, with 42 nations represented. Some 28 countries were members of the League of Nations throughout its existence. Another 35 either joined or withdrew during that time.

One of the most important aims of the League was to end the 'criminal threat of war', which had limited success. It oversaw the settlement of disputes between Finland and Sweden over the Åland Islands in 1921 and between Greece and Bulgaria over their mutual border in 1925. However, the Great Powers, such as Britain, France and Germany, chose to pursue their own foreign policies. This attitude, coupled with the lack of the United States as a member, severely limited the League's power.

Biography – Woodrow Wilson

(Thomas) Woodrow Wilson was the 28th president of the United States. He was born in Virginia and some of his earliest memories were of the hardships caused by the US Civil War (1861–65). Wilson was a brilliant scholar and taught at various colleges and universities, becoming president of Princeton University in 1890. He wrote extensively on politics and government and eventually entered politics himself, being elected governor of the state of New Jersey in 1911. The following year he was chosen to be the **Democratic** Party's candidate for US president, and he won that election. Wilson planned to introduce many reforms but he soon became involved in devising a US policy towards the First World War. He was re-elected in 1916 and the United States entered the war the following year.

Wilson helped to devise the peace agreement that ended the war and he introduced the notion of the League of Nations to act as a sort of parliament of nations. The US public and Congress, however, rejected further involvement in European affairs, so the United States never became a member. The Democratic Party chose a different candidate for the 1920 presidential election and Wilson retired from public office. He died in 1924.

President Wilson in France 1919.

'I can predict with absolute certainty that within another generation there will be another world war.'
Woodrow Wilson, 1919, trying to persuade US voters to join the League of Nations

Global conflict

By the 1930s Germany, Japan and Italy had embarked on an **expansionist** policy that seemed like an inevitable drift towards another war. It became apparent that the League of Nations was powerless to stop this, and its membership declined as a result. Germany's National Socialist (Nazi) government withdrew from the League in 1933. Japan also withdrew in 1933, after Japanese attacks on China were condemned. The League failed to stop the Italian conquest of Ethiopia, which began in 1935. The USSR, a member since 1934, was expelled following the Soviet attack on Finland in 1939.

Tanks cross the dry Ethiopian landscape during Italy's conquest of the country in 1935.

The Second World War

The next war, which Woodrow Wilson had predicted in his failed attempts to muster US support for the League of Nations, began in 1939. Over the course of the next six years it surpassed the First World War both in terms of bloodshed and in the use of the word 'world'. The Second World War was truly global, with for example naval engagements off South America, heavy fighting in Africa and fierce battles in Asia and the Pacific.

Soviet troops occupy Vyborg, on the Finnish-Soviet border during the 1939 conflict on the eve of the Second World War.

Some of the fighting resembled that of the First World War, with troops dug in and defending sites against other soldiers. But the war also saw many new developments in weaponry, which added significantly to the casualties and meant that millions of civilians were also killed and wounded. War now meant 'total war', and entire countries became battlefields. Air forces entered the modern age with the introduction of jet aircraft, while towards the end of the war Germany succeeded in launching powerful long-distance rockets against Britain. Most important, though, was the development by the United States of the atomic bomb. In 1945 the United States dropped two atomic bombs on Japan – on the cities of Hiroshima and Nagasaki. The effect was to force Japan to surrender almost immediately. In addition, though, the enormous destruction caused by the two bombs prompted many people to search for a way of ensuring that such weapons would never be used again. It was time to think again about peacekeeping.

> *'I climbed on top of a pile of corpses. Layer upon layer of them. Some were still moving, still alive. I had to get over them. I can still hear the cracking of their bones.'*
> **An eye-witness recalling Hiroshima years after the atomic bomb was dropped**

The birth of the United Nations

As the Second World War drew to a close it became apparent that it had been a war like no other. It dwarfed the First World War in terms of casualties – some 55 million people died, including civilians. Nazi Germany's 'Final Solution' had sent six million Jewish people to their death in a mass killing that has since become known as the Holocaust. Even before the world saw the results of the atomic bombs, people were horrified by the scale of the killing – and the scope for future **annihilation**.

Desperate and bewildered, the inmates of Buchenwald concentration camp provide evidence of Nazi Germany's cruelty, 1945.

With these thoughts in mind, representatives of 50 nations met in San Francisco in 1945 to sign a United Nations **charter** to replace the **covenant** of the League of Nations. In theory, the League had still been in existence, but the war had proved its fundamental weaknesses. The UN charter had a distinct advantage in this respect, in that the United States was a member. So too were the other major **Allied** countries that were to secure victory in the war – notably, the Soviet Union, Great Britain and China. The UN **charter** came into effect in October 1945, just two months after the Second World War ended. Although Japan only entered the UN in 1956 and Germany (by now divided into West and East) in 1973, the UN tried to ensure that the post-war settlement did not set out to cripple the countries that were defeated.

First steps for peace

The UN's first moves as a peacekeeping organization were in one of the world's most volatile areas – the Middle East. The area had erupted into violence in 1948, when a conflict arose between the Arab countries of the region and the new nation of Israel, created in accordance with a UN plan that **partitioned** Palestine into two separate states, one Jewish and one Arab. In 1949 a UN **mediator**, acting under the authority of the Security Council, negotiated a series of **armistice** agreements between Israel on the one hand, and Egypt, Jordan, Lebanon and Syria on the other. A United Nations Truce Supervision Organization (UNTSO) was formed to help the parties supervise the terms of the agreements.

The UN involvement in the Middle East, however, could hardly be called a triumph – many of the 600,000 Palestinian Arabs who had been displaced by the creation of Israel now lived in makeshift camps along Israel's border. Their sense of resentment, which echoed through the Arab world, would flare up on several more occasions. But for the time being, the UN could say that it had stopped the fighting as a first step towards peace.

An estimated 800,000 Arabs and Israelis benefited from the UN's emergency food supplies to Palestine in 1949.

The Cold War

The founding of the UN, which occurred in only a matter of months in 1945, reflected the sense of common purpose that the **Allied** powers had forged during the years spent fighting together in the Second World War. This sense of common interest, however, did not last long. Almost immediately after the war, it became apparent that the United States and the Soviet Union would be, at best, uneasy partners. These two countries had emerged at the end of the war as the world's dominant powers, and each had begun to distrust the other.

The reasons for this distrust can be seen clearly now. The **communist** system of government, in place in the Soviet Union since 1917, was bitterly opposed to the **free enterprise** economic approach of the United States. Communists hoped that workers around the world would follow the example of Russia and establish a communist government.

The United States feared the spread of communism in the immediate post-war period. From its point of view, the Soviet Union seemed to be turning many of the countries of Eastern Europe into communist **satellites**. The Soviet Union, having just lost 20 million people because of Germany's invasion during the Second World War, felt it needed to have a **buffer** of friendly allies to prevent future invasions. Moreover, the United States, France and Great Britain had already invaded the Soviet Union thirty years before in an effort to overturn the communist revolution. The Soviet Union maintained that they were capable of doing the same again.

By 1948 communist countries stretched down the whole of Eastern Europe, prompting Winston Churchill's 1946 statement that 'From Stettin in the Baltic to Trieste in the Adriatic, an iron curtain has descended across the continent.' The United States and western European countries feared further advances and established **NATO** as a military alliance in 1949. In the same year, the Soviet Union developed its first atomic weapons, ending the advantage that the United States had held since the end of the Second World War. The Soviet Union, along with its communist neighbours, established the **Warsaw Pact** as a response to NATO in 1955.

The Bikini hydrogen bomb test, 1952. By the end of the 1950s five countries had the power to destroy the world many times over.

Uneasy peace

With both of the world's **superpowers** now armed with atomic weapons, the prospects for world peace seemed poor. Both countries used the forum of the UN to make savage attacks on the other. With their superior economic and military influence, the superpowers could also enlist the aid of their allies in many UN votes.

This period of tension and hostility, known as the **Cold War**, harmed the UN and frustrated its many efforts to engage in peacekeeping over the next four decades. One of the main reasons was that the superpowers, fearing a direct atomic war with each other, resorted to furthering their interests by supporting elements in many conflicts. Either the United States or the Soviet Union could **veto** UN involvement if it felt that the conflict concerned their own interests.

Soviet leader Nikita Khrushchev, seen here addressing the UN General Assembly in 1960, was a key figure during the tense Cold War period.

War by proxy

Many of the conflicts that arose after the Second World War involved countries that had once been **colonies** of European powers. From the late 1940s onwards, these countries – mainly in Africa and Asia – were struggling to achieve or maintain their own independence.

Both the United States and Soviet Union tried to influence the course of this process by sending arms or other assistance to the political groups that were gaining power in these newly independent countries. Sometimes they aided **guerrilla** factions that were trying to overthrow one of these new governments.

The **superpowers** would rarely send in their own troops for fear of drawing their counterpart into outright war. Using the conflicts of other people as a means of furthering one's own interests is called fighting a war by **proxy**, and thousands of lives were lost during the **Cold War** in these type of struggles.

One of the most dramatic instances of such a conflict has been in the Middle East. Although the UN had been involved there since 1949, both superpowers took a direct interest in dictating the course of affairs. The United States pumped billions of dollars – as well as vast amounts of weaponry – into Israel, while the Soviet Union provided similar assistance for Israel's Arab enemies.

There were two tragic and disastrous examples of direct superpower involvement in other countries' affairs. In each case, the UN was powerless to do anything apart from issue the occasional **denunciation**. The United States was involved for two decades in supporting the anti-**communist** government of South Vietnam in its war against communist North Vietnam. The involvement failed when North Vietnamese troops defeated South Vietnam in April 1975. More than 2 million Vietnamese had lost their lives, along with nearly 58,000 US troops.

In the second example, Soviet troops spent much of the 1980s involved in an ultimately fruitless attempt to support a communist government in Afghanistan against Muslim rebels. Estimates of casualties in this fighting, including those of Soviet forces, range from 700,000 to 1.3 million.

'A world organization has already been erected for the prime purpose of preventing war. UNO [United Nations Organization], the successor of the League of Nations, with the decisive addition of the United States and all that that means, is already at work. We must make sure that its work is fruitful, that it is a reality and not a sham, that it is a force for action and not merely a frothing of words.'
Winston Churchill, 1946

Turning point: Korea

The **Cold War** entered a new phase in 1949, when **communist** troops, led by Mao Zedong, overthrew the government in China. China's huge population, consisting mainly of peasant farmers, welcomed the new communist government, but the Chinese revolution had a more complicated effect on the international scene. The United States, in particular, did not welcome the emergence of a huge new ally of the Soviet Union.

It did not take long for the initial tension to develop into outright conflict. The setting was the country of Korea, a peninsula extending south-east from China. Korea had been under Japanese control during the Second World War but after the war it had been divided – like Germany in Europe. The Soviets supported the North and helped set up a communist government there. The government of the South favoured the United States.

On 25 June 1950 the North Korean army attacked the South. US President Harry Truman immediately protested to the UN Security Council, which called for North Korean troops to leave South Korea. Further Security Council resolutions called for UN members to supply troops to repel the attack on South Korea. The Security Council agreement came swiftly because the Soviet representative had left the Council in protest at the UN's failure to recognize the new Chinese government.

Military action

President Truman sent combat forces to Korea, where they were later joined by troops from Australia, Belgium, Luxembourg, Canada, Colombia, Ethiopia, France, Greece, the Netherlands, New Zealand, the Philippines, South Africa, Thailand, Turkey and the UK. These forces were placed under a unified UN command headed by the US commander in chief in the Far East, General Douglas MacArthur. Medical units from Denmark, India and Sweden completed the UN group. It was to be the first instance of the UN using military action to repel an attack. Truman and other leaders were eager not to repeat the failure of the League of Nations, which had been unable to deal with similar attacks.

Fighting began almost immediately, with North Korean forces capturing nearly all of the peninsula. By September, however, the tide turned. UN troops made a daring **amphibious** landing about halfway up the peninsula and managed to cut off the North Korean army to the south. More than 140,000 North Koreans were killed or captured and MacArthur decided to cross the border into the north in order to reunite the country.

General Douglas MacArthur (seated) favoured an all-out war against his communist enemies during the Korean conflict.

Playing for high stakes

Up to this point the UN forces had encountered only North Korean military units, although these units were largely supplied by the Soviet Union. China had stayed out of the conflict. But as UN troops swept northward into North Korea, China warned that it would enter the war unless these troops retreated south of the border. On 15 October 1950 General MacArthur was asked if he felt that there was any danger of China entering the war, and he replied 'Very little.' The very next day some 300,000 Chinese troops crossed into Korea.

The Chinese action was partly to aid a **communist** neighbour but it also had an element of self-defence. China considered the UN action to be a US military adventure and it knew that many US military leaders wanted to overthrow the new communist government in China.

Scottish soldiers, part of the UK's contribution to the UN effort, take cover during fighting in 1950.

So it was with a spirit of national pride that the Chinese forces took on the UN troops. The pendulum began to swing back as the Chinese cut off UN troops in the north and went on to capture Seoul (the South Korean capital) on 4 January 1951.

But as with the previous advances – by both sides in the conflict – the troops had spread themselves too thinly. The UN forces were able once more to cut off supply lines, this time extending into China, and to regain some of the lost territory. But, as with the previous advances, it was the Korean civilian population that suffered. As well as being overrun by foot soldiers, the Koreans had to deal with heavy **artillery** and aerial bombing.

The renewed UN effort pushed the Chinese forces northwards once more. By 22 April 1951 they were north of the original border; at the same time, the remaining UN forces in the north moved southwards across the same border. By July both sides began a series of peace talks. The negotiations were bad-tempered at first but gradually the two sides agreed to sign an **armistice** on 27 July 1953.

The fighting had ended, but the war had cost 1,820,000 lives and enormous amounts of money. The UN had shown itself to be a force to be reckoned with, although it had entered the conflict without the agreement of one of its most powerful members. Moreover, many countries saw the Korean conflict as less of a peacekeeping operation than a chance for smaller countries to suffer because of the **Cold War**. This aspect became more alarming when it emerged that General MacArthur, who was relieved of command in April 1951, had wanted to use atomic weapons against the Chinese. It was unlikely that the UN could play a successful peacekeeping role without resolving some of the questions that the Korean experience had raised.

Counting the cost

Seventeen member nations suffered casualties in the UN operation in Korea. Almost one million South Koreans were killed or wounded. It is difficult to measure Chinese and North Korean casualties, but it has been estimated that there were around 900,000 Chinese killed or wounded. Half a century later, the Korean peninsula remains divided.

The 'Blue Helmets'

In order to become a member of the UN, a country must promise to be 'peace-loving', and the safeguarding of international peace has been a key UN objective since its foundation in 1945. The UN **charter** gives the responsibility of maintaining peace to the Security Council. And since five of the permanent members of the Security Council – China, Russia, France, the United Kingdom and the United States – have the power to **veto** any decision on peacekeeping operations, there can often be some tricky negotiations before an operation can begin.

The UN Security council met in special session to try to end the Iran–Iraq war, which dragged on through most of the 1980s.

But although the UN exists largely to promote and preserve peace, it has no army of its own and cannot send troops to stabilize every conflict that arises around the world. It relies on member states to supply both troops and equipment for the operations. Several factors limit the UN in this respect. The first, as mentioned above, concerns diplomacy. Although the world is no longer constrained by **Cold War** limitations – at that time vetoes were both common and predictable – some permanent members might not agree to send in a force. Another limitation is more obvious. The UN can only send in a peacekeeping force if the two parties in a dispute agree to it.

Into conflict

Having agreed to authorize a peacekeeping operation, the Security Council must decide on specific goals for the mission. Ideally, the UN would say 'bring peace to Eastern Europe, Central Africa, (or wherever)', but the mission can only succeed if it has a special **mandate**. This sets out clearly defined purposes for the peacekeeping mission. And backing up this mandate is a special peacekeeping budget to reimburse participating countries.

The governments that have volunteered the use of their troops retain command of their soldiers throughout the mission. These soldiers wear their own national uniforms, but they also wear blue berets or helmets with the UN insignia. This headwear is instantly recognizable and is a source of pride for the soldiers who wear it, who are often referred to as the 'Blue Helmets' or the 'Blue Berets'.

A Kenyan UN peacekeeper and his Dutch comrade give refreshment to an elderly Bosnian woman during fighting in 1995.

The presence of UN peacekeeping forces is often enough to calm things down, and the UN forces are generally only lightly armed for self-defence. Sometimes, though, their weapons must be used and they do suffer casualties. About 1600 UN military and civilian personnel have died in the performance of their duties since 1948.

Apart from their military role, UN peacekeepers conduct a number of political, medical and humanitarian activities as part of their mission. Election observers, medical staff and **human-rights** monitors work alongside the soldiers in many cases. Their job is to help an area return to normal, ultimately with free elections and human rights. In the meantime they must try to make a place safe for its inhabitants by finding temporary housing for refugees, clearing landmines and training police forces to maintain order.

'How do you conduct an election where there is little, if any, tradition of free and fair elections; where media is tightly controlled; where nobody in the community is registered yet? The first step was an enormous publicity push to encourage all local residents to get their citizenship papers and to convince them that voting was the only effective way to have their voices heard.'
A peacekeeper from the United Nations Transitional Administration in Eastern Slavonia, Baranja and Western Sirmium, 1996

'There is more shooting going on now, the crack of rounds flying past your head is becoming commonplace. The locals are beginning to get restless … It is unbearably hot here. Every day is 55°C (132°F) in the shade. It is always 55° because that is as high as our thermometers go. The ration of a few litres of warm water we get every day is barely enough. Our clothes are stained with the salt of our sweat mixed with the red dust of the desert. We spend as much of the day as possible under cover, moving as little as possible. Only in the evening do we emerge from our holes, safe from the blistering heat of the sun.'
From the journal of a Canadian peacekeeper in Somalia, 1993

Enforcement

Not all troops representing the UN are involved in peacekeeping operations. For a UN military operation to be termed 'peacekeeping' it must have the agreement of both parties. There have been occasions, however, when the Security Council has become alarmed by the spread of a conflict and has authorized troops to be despatched even without the agreement of the warring parties. Such an operation is described as an enforcement action, as opposed to a peacekeeping mission. An enforcement operation is not under UN control. Instead, the UN agrees to let a single country, or a group of countries, direct the operation. UN operations in Korea (see pages 18–21), the Gulf War (see pages 38–41), Somalia, Haiti and Albania were actually enforcement missions. Such missions must follow the same UN **charter** provisions for the maintenance of peace and security.

UN peacekeepers from Australia patrol Dili, East Timor, during their mission to restore peace in 1999.

Turning point: Suez

The Middle East was the first area in which UN peacekeeping operations were undertaken and the region has remained a 'hot spot' ever since. Many factors underlie this complex international problem, including Israel's relations with its Arab neighbours, the continued flow of international oil supplies, and world fears about terrorism.

These factors were already important in the 1950s; in addition, the Middle East threatened to be an arena for Cold War **antagonism**. It was midway through that decade that a major international conflict developed concerning the Suez Canal, which connects the Mediterranean Sea and the Red Sea, giving access to the Indian Ocean. The canal provides a shortcut for ships operating between both European and American ports and ports located in southern Asia, eastern Africa and Oceania. The Suez Canal, which runs through Egypt, had been built by a company with British and French funding in the 1860s and the same company operated the Suez Canal in the 1950s.

With such a strategic location the Suez Canal assumed great importance in the 20th century. The United Kingdom and Egypt had signed a treaty in 1936 allowing British warships to patrol the canal approaches. This arrangement enabled British naval forces to pass freely though the Suez Canal throughout the Second World War. A new treaty in 1954 called for the withdrawal of the British military presence and by June 1956 the withdrawal was complete. The following month Egypt decided to **nationalize** the dam; this move would mean that Egypt would receive the transit fees paid by all ships passing through the canal. President Gamal Abdel Nasser announced that Egypt planned to use the proceeds from the operation of the canal to finance an expensive Aswan High Dam project.

'We believe in international law. But we will never submit. We shall show the world how a small country can stand in the face of great powers threatening with armed might. Egypt might be a small power, but she is great inasmuch as she has faith in her power and convictions.'
Egypt's President Nasser speaking during the Suez Crisis, 15 September 1956

Full-scale invasion

The nationalization of the Suez Canal was welcomed by Egyptians and many in the Arab world, who saw Nasser as a powerful figure who could become a force for unity. France and the United Kingdom, however, were furious. Both of these countries stood to lose a great deal of money because of the nationalization. Israel, at the same time, was planning an invasion because Arab commandos from Egypt had been raiding Israel. It was clear that three countries – France, the United Kingdom and Israel – had a common interest. Representatives of the three governments held secret meetings in October 1956.

On 29 October 1956, Israel invaded Egypt. Two days later, British and French military units attacked Egypt for the announced purpose of ensuring free passage through the canal. In retaliation, Egypt sank 40 ships in the canal, effectively blocking it. In fierce fighting the Israelis pushed through the Sinai Peninsula to the canal, while French and British soldiers defeated Egyptian troops along the canal.

Egyptians crowd round a British tank after UK forces invaded Egypt in 1956 in an effort to reopen the Suez Canal.

A united UN

The invasion was a military success but a **propaganda** nightmare, at least for France and the United Kingdom. Six years earlier, during the Korean Conflict, the UN had approved the 'Uniting for Peace' resolution, which enabled the UN General Assembly to continue discussing a case that had been **vetoed** by a Security Council member. In 1956, the United States – along with the Soviet Union and a vast majority of UN member-states – had disapproved of the Suez invasion. Using the 'Uniting for Peace' provision, the General Assembly passed a series of resolutions calling for an end to the fighting. It also set up a United Nations Emergency Force (UNEF) to ensure and supervise compliance by the countries involved.

The extent of the international disapproval came as something of a surprise for France and the United Kingdom, which now realized that they could no longer intervene in the internal affairs of smaller countries.

UN peacekeepers, seen here in 1955, have been a constant feature of Middle East life since the 1940s.

Through the intervention of the UN, a truce was arranged in November, and by the end of the year Israeli, French and British forces were withdrawn from the area. Following removal of the sunken vessels by a UN salvage team, the Egyptian government reopened the canal in March 1957.

The Suez Crisis had shown that, far from letting a conflict develop into a **Cold War** confrontation, the UN could draw on the support of the two **superpowers** to enforce a peace. Two former **imperial** powers, France and the United Kingdom, had been forced to bow to a new international force for peace.

Wider allegiances

Many historians have seen the Suez Crisis as the last gasp of imperialism and the dawn of a new international order. Supporting this claim is the behaviour of Canada, a former British **colony** and loyal member of the **Commonwealth**. When Canadian Prime Minister Louis Stephen St Laurent learned of the invasion, he sent a cable to London, stating his disapproval of what he considered an immoral and irresponsible act. He gave Lester Pearson, Canada's Ambassador to the UN, a free hand in trying to bring about an immediate **ceasefire**. Pearson's historic resolution calling for the establishment of an immediate truce and the dispatch of a UN peacekeeping force was accepted. To back up the UN decision, St Laurent immediately made available Canadian troops, which were sent to the troubled area. Pearson who, with St Laurent, had also been involved in the founding of the UN, was awarded the Nobel Peace Prize in 1957.

End of Empires

Much of the UN's peacekeeping work, from the Suez Crisis to the break-up of Yugoslavia in the 1990s, has been in areas where people are struggling for independence. On 14 December 1960 the UN General Assembly committed itself to the end of colonialism 'in all its forms' stating: 'All peoples have the right to self-determination; by virtue of that right they freely determine their political status and freely pursue their economic, social and cultural development.'

Turning point: the Congo

The Suez Crisis had increased the international standing of the UN, in its role as a peacekeeping organization. Although **Cold War** tensions continued to simmer, the UN had shown itself to be an organization that could command the respect – and compliance – of all its members. In particular, the crisis had shown that the UN was an effective forum for discussing matters relating to the end of the **imperial** system around the world.

Nowhere was this subject more heated than in Africa. The Second World War had left the great European imperial powers – mainly the United Kingdom, France, Belgium and Italy – weakened. They had their own countries to rebuild and had little money left to support expensive empires. In addition, neither of the two **superpowers**, the United States and the Soviet Union, had ever owned African territories. Each in its own way opposed imperialism and was likely to support independence movements in Africa's former European **colonies**.

A troubled beginning

Some former colonies, such as Ghana (under British control) and Côte d'Ivoire (Ivory Coast: under French control) achieved independence in the 1950s after forming more or less united political organizations. Others, divided by tribal conflict or **oppressive** land-ownership systems, became unstable and found the transition to independence much more difficult. The most dramatic example of this type of nation was the Congo.

The Congo, a huge country in the heart of central Africa, had been a Belgian colony since the 19th century. The Belgians had benefited from the Congo's immense natural resources, especially its mineral wealth. But the local people, known as the Congolese, had little say in how their country was run and had virtually no chance of becoming educated. The Belgians began to introduce reforms in the late 1950s, but the impatient Congolese, demanding independence, rioted in Léopoldville (the capital) in 1959.

The Belgian government then announced a schedule for Congolese elections, which were to establish self-rule. But, after pressure from leading nationalist parties, Belgium agreed to grant full independence. In elections held prior to independence, Patrice Lumumba, of the Congolese National Movement, was elected Premier-designate and Joseph Kasavubu, of the Abako Party, became President. The Independent Republic of the Congo was proclaimed in Léopoldville on 30 June 1960.

Armed revolt

Within days the country was thrown into chaos as tribal groups clashed and the Congolese armed forces revolted. Then, on 11 July, the mineral-rich Katanga Province declared its own independence and requested Belgian military aid. Some Belgian military troops had remained in the Congo to protect the property of Europeans still living there.

Patrice Lumumba (smiling) arrives at London airport in 1960 on his way to put his case to the United Nations in New York.

Lumumba feared that Belgium would recognize and support the independence of Katanga and try to regain control in the Congo. He appealed to the United Nations Security Council, which authorized Secretary-General Dag Hammarskjöld to recruit a military force to be sent to the Congo to restore order; the Security Council also demanded withdrawal of Belgian forces. The UN force, comprising units from African countries, Sweden, and Ireland, gradually began to replace Belgian troops. When the Security Council ruled that no UN forces should be used to affect the outcome of any internal conflict in the province, the rulers of Katanga allowed UN troops to enter.

UN peacekeepers from Ireland played a vital role in the confused and violent struggle in the Congo in the early 1960s.

A complex mandate

The next four years saw a bitter and confusing civil war, during which Lumumba was murdered by his own army. The UN had a complicated mission, trying to restore order and prevent civil war within the Congo as a whole and to **implement** some sort of solution to the Katanga problem. It was during a mission to mediate in the Katanga dispute that UN Secretary-General Dag Hammarskjöld died in a plane crash in September 1961.

During the first half of 1962, UN Secretary-General U Thant proposed a three-stage plan for ending Katanga's **secession**. Moise Tshombe, leader of Katanga, announced his acceptance of the plan but made little effort to implement it. In December 1962, UN forces moved decisively against Katanga and gained control of Elisabethville, its capital. This settled the matter of Katanga – at least in military terms – and peacekeepers concentrated on restoring order to the reunited Congo.

The mission ended in June 1964, just as a new constitution was taking effect. The Congo (called Zaire between 1971 and 1999) was to remain unstable for many years to come, and it later descended into a one-party **dictatorship**, but the UN involvement had prevented a much more devastating conflict from engulfing the country. Just as importantly, the UN's first peacekeeping involvement in Africa sent a message to other countries and indirectly smoothed the transition to independence in other former **colonies**.

Biography – Dag Hammarskjöld

Dag Hjalmar Agne Carl Hammarskjöld was born in Jönköping, Sweden, on 29 July 1905, and educated at the universities of Uppsala and Stockholm. He entered politics and later the diplomatic service as a finance specialist in the Swedish foreign office. Hammarskjöld was the chief of the Swedish delegation to the UN in 1952 and early 1953. On 7 April 1953, he was elected UN Secretary-General, succeeding Trygve Lie of Norway.

UN Secretary-General Dag Hammarskjöld reviews Swedish troops in the Congo, 1960.

Hammarskjöld raised the profile of his office and travelled greatly to further the ends of the UN. He gained the respect of both the United States and the Soviet Union during the height of the **Cold War** and was widely respected for his skills as a negotiator. It was on one of these negotiating trips – to try to arrange an end to the Katanga fighting in the Congo – that he died in a plane crash in Ndola, Northern Rhodesia (now Zambia) in September 1961. In recognition of his statesmanship and contributions to peace, Hammarskjöld was **posthumously** awarded the Nobel Peace Prize in 1961.

Keeping things cool

While UN peacekeeping operations often dominate the world headlines – in the former Yugoslavia in the mid-1990s, in East Timor in 1999 and in Sierra Leone in 2000 – many UN missions carry on with less fanfare. With no troops in the firing line, these operations might seem less newsworthy, but they work to the same end of bringing peace to a region. In fact, such operations allow the UN to plan more carefully how to set up a mission, rather than rushing in when a conflict has already blown out of control. Such missions were a favourite of UN Secretary-General Dag Hammarskjöld, who greatly favoured what he termed 'preventive diplomacy'. This strategy had two main purposes: to help 'cool things down' if necessary as a first step, and then to help with the peaceful rebuilding of **democratic** institutions.

As a result, many UN peacekeeping missions remain in an area for a number of years, long after the fighting has stopped. And while the UN retains a blue-helmeted military presence in the region – acting as a deterrent to further fighting – the real activity shifts its focus to civilian affairs.

The 'Blue Berets' have spent nearly 40 years on Cyprus, trying to reduce tensions between the Greek and Turkish communities.

Case study: Cyprus

Cyprus, the fourth largest island in the Mediterranean Sea, has had a remarkably troubled history. Its location in the eastern Mediterranean has made it strategically important for more than 3000 years. During that time it has been conquered or ruled by many **imperial** powers, notably Egypt, Assyria, Persia, Greece, England, Venice, Turkey and Great Britain. Despite the diversity of those who have ruled Cyprus, the island's population comes mainly from two traditions – Greek (80 per cent) and Turkish (18 per cent).

The recent history of Cyprus has focused on conflict between these two groups. Turkey had lost control of Cyprus after the First World War and believed it should regain its rule when the British were planning to depart in the 1950s. The Greek Cypriots, for their part, wanted to unite with Greece. After bad-tempered negotiations, Cyprus became independent in 1960 and elected a Greek president and Turkish vice-president. Tensions flared almost immediately as the Turkish Cypriots wanted to **partition** the island and Greek Cypriots wanted to strengthen their control over a unified Cyprus. Serious fighting erupted between these two groups.

The UN sent in a peacekeeping force in March 1964 and persuaded both sides to agree to a **ceasefire** on 10 August 1964. This move did not remove the problem – or even lessen the emotions on either side – but it prevented a full-scale civil war from erupting on the island. The peacekeeping force numbered 7000 troops at its peak, but has been gradually reduced in the decades since independence.

The UN force has been severely tested, especially when fighting broke out again in 1974. Turkey sent in troops to support Turkish Cypriots, but the UN supervised a division of the island and helped resettle 8000 Turkish Cypriots in the northern half. The Turkish Cypriots declared their part of Cyprus independent in 1983, but the UN refuses to recognize this move and continues to patrol the border.

Case study: Western Sahara

In 1975 Morocco occupied the former Spanish **colony** of Western Sahara despite widespread international protests. Neighbouring Mauritania also claimed part of the former colony but withdrew this claim after a **guerrilla** campaign mounted by the inhabitants of Western Sahara. The group behind the campaign is known as the Polisario Front, which seeks to establish an independent country, free of outside control.

In 1975, Morocco's King Hassan encouraged Moroccan settlement of Western Sahara by ordering the Green March of 350,000 people. This move triggered fierce fighting between Morocco and the Polisario Front, which intensified when the Organization for African Unity (OAU) recognized the independent country in 1983.

The UN sent in a peacekeeping force in 1991 and worked out a peace plan, which led to a truce in September 1991. The UN force remains, awaiting the outcome of a **referendum** on self-determination. However, this referendum has been postponed repeatedly due to disagreements over the number of Western Saharan people eligible to vote.

A French peacekeeper discusses a Western Sahara peace plan with Polisario Commander Mouloud, 1991.

Case study: Haiti

Haiti comprises about half of Hispaniola (the other half is the Dominican Republic), the largest island in the Caribbean Sea. It is one of the poorest countries in the world, with a history of brutal **dictatorships**. It became a focus of world attention in the 1980s, as reformers in Haiti tried to introduce a **democratic** government. Internationally supervised elections held in December 1990 resulted in a landslide presidential victory for Jean-Bertrand Aristide, a Roman Catholic priest and an outspoken supporter of the poor.

Aristide, however, was **deposed** by the Haitian military, a move that prompted the UN to introduce a series of measures to force Haiti to restore Aristide and his democratically elected government. By 1994, the UN had called for member-states to use all necessary means – including military – to restore democracy. The United States sent in 20,000 troops and the military government stepped down. In early 1995 the US troops were replaced by a UN peacekeeping force, which tried to maintain order while the country returned to democratic rule.

The UN force has had many tasks in achieving this aim, most important of which has been establishing a police force that would respect human rights and would have the respect of the population. The UN has carefully helped as this force has been formed, and its last task before leaving in 2000 was to complete a period of monitoring.

The UN headquarters in New York City.

Turning point: the Gulf War

The events in 1991 that became known as the Gulf War were significant in many ways, even though this massive operation cannot be described as a 'traditional' UN peacekeeping effort. For a start, it marked the first test of international co-operation in the era after the end of the **Cold War**. The Soviet Union was fragmenting, soon to be replaced by a number of non-**communist** countries. Whereas in the decades of the Cold War, the Soviet Union would automatically **veto** any action being led by the United States, in the case of the Gulf War the Soviets voiced no objections. And secondly, the scale of the operation called for the largest concentration of soldiers and weaponry amassed since the end of the Second World War. If the United States was to return to its role as 'the world's policeman' – unchallenged by a rival **superpower** – it wanted to show that it had backing for large-scale operations.

The question of oil

At its heart, the Gulf War involved two countries – Iraq and Kuwait – but more importantly it concerned the flow of oil. Both Iraq and Kuwait are major oil producers, and their economies rely on earning as much as possible from their oil exports. Iraq had spent much of the 1980s at war with its neighbour Iran, and the experience had proved very costly. Iraq needed its oil **revenue** more than ever by 1990 in order to rebuild itself. It was then that Iraq turned its attention to its smaller southern neighbour, Kuwait. Although Kuwait had supported Iraq during the war with Iran, Iraq had always considered Kuwait to be one of its own provinces. Things came to a head in 1990 when Iraq claimed that Kuwait was exporting too much oil, thereby lowering the price of oil world-wide and injuring Iraq's economy.

Operation Desert Storm

The crisis began in August 1990, when Iraq, led by President Saddam Hussein, invaded and **annexed** Kuwait. This move brought swift condemnation from the international community. Between August and November the UN Security Council passed a series of resolutions that culminated in the demand that Iraq withdraw **unconditionally** from Kuwait by 15 January 1991. Several of the Security Council permanent members – the United States, the United Kingdom and France – depended on oil from the region and they were concerned that the flow of oil would become unpredictable.

Iraqi President Saddam Hussein visits a military training camp during the Gulf War, 1991.

The UN also stated that member-states could use whatever means necessary to remove Iraqi forces from Kuwait if the deadline passed. The United States took the lead in building up a military force that would perform this task – turning the Kuwait question into one of enforcement, like that in Korea 40 years before. By the time of the deadline, some 500,000 allied ground, air, and naval forces personnel – chiefly from the United States, Saudi Arabia, Great Britain, Egypt, Syria and France – were grouped against an Iraqi army estimated at that time to number 540,000.

Under the command of US General H Norman Schwarzkopf, the multinational **coalition** began the military operation known as Operation Desert Storm. The coalition used its superior airpower to bomb military targets in Iraq and Kuwait within 24 hours of the UN deadline expiring. The planes used advanced weaponry such as laser-guided bombs and cruise missiles, as well as less sophisticated conventional weapons. Having achieved this initial aim, Schwarzkopf's forces turned to knocking out Iraq's communications centres, thereby making it difficult for the Iraqis to issue commands from their capital, Baghdad.

During their retreat from Kuwait in March 1991, Iraqi troops set fire to many oil wells, which burned out of control for weeks.

Forced into peace

Still operating with full UN backing, the **coalition** spent several weeks bombing Baghdad and other major Iraqi cities, while ground troops – also equipped with high-tech weaponry – defeated the Iraqi infantry positioned along the Iraq-Kuwait border. Iraq suffered terrible losses among both civilians and soldiers during this fighting and by mid-February began to indicate that it would withdraw from Kuwait.

Iraqi representatives accepted allied coalition's terms for a provisional truce on 3 March and a permanent **ceasefire** on 6 April. Iraq agreed to pay **reparations** to Kuwait, reveal the location and extent of its stockpiles of chemical and biological weapons, and eliminate its weapons of mass destruction. The UN set up a group – the United Nations Iraq-Kuwait Observer Mission (UNIKOM) – to monitor the border and to check on Iraq's **decommissioning** of weapons. UNIKOM observers remain in Iraq, but over the years they have voiced complaints that the Iraqi government was frustrating their attempts to monitor Iraqi compliance.

Lingering doubts

Operation Desert Storm achieved its aims in a matter of weeks, but the operation raised doubts among many people. Some countries at the UN argued that the Security Council only sprang into action because of their members' own concerns about keeping oil flowing from the important Middle East region. They pointed to border disputes around the world where no UN forces had been mobilized. Others were more realistic, accepting that the United States needed to prove its military worth after suffering humiliation in its twenty-year struggle to quash **communism** in Vietnam. Whether they approved or not, however, nearly every observer agreed with President George Bush when he forecast a 'new world order' in dealing with international disputes.

'What is at stake is more than one small country, it is a big idea – a new world order, where diverse nations are drawn together in a common cause to achieve the universal aspirations of mankind; peace and security, freedom and the rule of law.'
George Bush, 1991

UN weapons inspectors return to Baghdad in 1998 in an effort to monitor Iraq's ability to mount another attack.

Turning point: Yugoslavia

The first half of the 1990s saw the UN involved in one of its largest ever peacekeeping operations as well as a number of spin-off missions, in an area that has long been subject to bitter conflicts and warfare. The operations took place in the different countries that had made up a larger country known as Yugoslavia. This area of south-eastern Europe is sometimes called the Balkans, after the mountain range that runs through its southern region.

Taking apart the jigsaw puzzle

The first shots of the First World War were fired around the Serbian city of Belgrade in July 1914. That war diminished the strength and influence of the foreign powers that had controlled much of the area, and the next 25 years saw moves for these various nations to unite as a single, independent country. This aim was realized in 1946 when the Federal People's Republic of Yugoslavia was formed. The new country comprised six republics: Bosnia-Herzegovina, Croatia, Macedonia, Montenegro, Serbia and Slovenia.

Following on from the strong leadership of its first Premier, Josip Broz Tito, Yugoslavia remained united well into the 1980s. The differences in culture, religion and ethnic background of its different republics were played down in favour of the greater power that the united country could have. Yugoslavia pursued a socialist economic policy but, by the late 1980s, several of the republics wanted more independence. They saw the decline of the **communist** system elsewhere in Eastern Europe and they also feared the increasing power of the republic of Serbia within their own country. Things came to a head in 1991 when the republics of Slovenia, Macedonia and Croatia declared their independence. Yugoslavia had begun to unravel.

A complex conflict

Slovenia and Macedonia achieved independence with little opposition but a serious conflict broke out in Croatia almost immediately. Many Serbs lived inside this newly independent country and the republic of Serbia sent weapons to help these Serbs fight to establish a Serbian state within Croatia. In September 1991 the UN imposed an arms **embargo** to stop arms from reaching the former republics of Yugoslavia.

**Serbian troops examine the desolated landscape
of Croatia during the civil war of 1991.**

In February 1992 the UN sent a peacekeeping force – the United
Nations Protection Force (UNPROFOR) – to the Serb-controlled
areas of Croatia. Its job, at first, was to ensure that three 'United
Nations Protected Areas' were free of military action and to
control their borders. This job proved difficult as the conflict in
the former Yugoslavia worsened. In June it spread to Bosnia-
Herzegovina, prompting the UN to widen UNPROFOR's **mandate**
to ensure the security of the airport at Sarajevo. The residents of
that city were under constant bombardment and the UN force
tried to keep them supplied with essential food and medical
supplies. The world watched with horror and confusion, trying to
understand the complex reasons for the fierce fighting.

Bitter disputes

The conflict in Bosnia had similar roots to those in Croatia. As in Croatia, there were many Serbs living in the republic. When Bosnia-Herzegovina declared its independence in early 1992 the heavily armed Bosnian Serbs occupied more than 60 per cent of the republic. They expelled – and sometimes murdered – thousands of Muslims and Croats from these areas in a process known as **ethnic cleansing**.

As the conflict in Bosnia grew worse, the situation in Croatia become somewhat clearer. Croatian forces, over the next few years, gradually recaptured most of their territory. The Serbs living in these areas fled to neighbouring Serbia or south into Bosnia, where the fighting continued.

In effect, the Bosnian conflict had become a civil war within a civil war. UNPROFOR monitored the many convoys of displaced civilians there – Serbs leaving Croatia as well as Bosnian Muslims and Croats leaving Bosnian Serb-held territories.

The UN also designated six Bosnian cities, including Sarajevo, as 'safe areas', which UNPROFOR undertook to protect. In performing this task, the UN force co-operated with the International Red Cross (in protecting civilians) and with **NATO**, which had imposed a 'no-fly zone' across much of Bosnia in an attempt to contain the conflict.

Serbian President Slobodan Milosevic led his country into several costly military involvements after the break-up of Yugoslavia in 1990.

By 1994 the UNPROFOR force consisted of more than 24,000 troops. It could claim some successes, such as monitoring the 1994 **ceasefire** between Bosnian Muslims and Croats. However, the UN force came in for criticism that its commanders were unwilling to protect the 'safe areas' against Serbian attacks. Moreover, more than one million people had been displaced in the process of ethnic cleansing. Fierce fighting had forced another million to leave their homes.

Picking up the pieces

The tide of war eventually turned away from the Serbs, and UNPROFOR monitored a ceasefire between Bosnian Serbs and the Bosnian government which took effect on 1 January 1995. A peace plan, known as the Dayton Accord, was signed two months later. The fighting wound down and UNPROFOR was disbanded in December 1995. The UN, however, set up several new peacekeeping forces to help various former republics of Yugoslavia – primarily Croatia and Bosnia – to recover and become peaceful once again. These remain in place, and have been joined by a separate peacekeeping force in the Serbian province of Kosovo, which saw a bitter conflict in 1999.

The bitter conflict in Bosnia left many families homeless after being forced from their villages by Serbian troops.

The role of the media

'Truth is the first casualty', is the journalist's saying about reporting events during a war. This means that, due to pressures of national interest, morale and outright **propaganda**, a reporter is limited in what he or she can say about the success or failure of armed forces. Although this sentiment is a sad one for anyone interested in the truth, it is also understandable. A country often needs to control some of its normal freedoms in order to unite against a common enemy.

The story should be very different for peacekeepers, however. The UN, with its emphasis on unity and consensus, takes great pains to remain neutral in the disputes it tries to resolve. In this respect, it should welcome any media interest that seeks to support this even-handed stance. However, the situation is far more complex than that, and the UN peacekeepers have often been subject to harsh – and even misleading – news reporting. Just how much this condemnation is justified, and how much reflects a political bias on the part of the media, is a matter for debate. The truth is that every branch of the UN is aware of the need to justify its running costs, and in the case of the peacekeepers it must also account for loss of life among troops from participating countries. A good relationship with the world media is the only real way to put its case to the people that matter – the world's public.

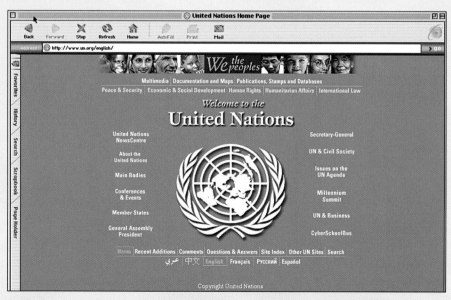

The United Nations website reflects the importance of public awareness in the age of the Internet.

Mastering the message

The telecommunications revolution has increased the flow of information and at the same time made it harder to control that flow. In general, this should be good news for the UN peacekeepers, since a fuller picture can emerge from each conflict that they enter. The experience of the Gulf War is a case in point. While journalists based with the UN-sponsored **coalition** faced narrow reporting restrictions, other reporters – notably satellite television broadcasters – based in Iraq could offer a different perspective. The Internet is another area of interest. Many websites provide in-depth information about peacekeeping – its history, successes and failures. At the same time the UN uses its own website (www.un.org) to provide a full range of information about its efforts, providing ample support for its argument that peacekeeping is an efficient and inexpensive way to maintain world peace. The Internet presence is just one aspect of the UN's Department of Public Information, which recognizes 'the increasing awareness of the importance of public information in peacekeeping, both as a security element and as a tool to achieve mission goals'.

Cold War echoes

The UN had the widespread support of its member-states upon its foundation in 1945. This attitude, shared by elements in the press on both sides of the **Cold War** divide, continued as the UN embarked on its first peacekeeping role in the Middle East in 1948. By remaining firm and impartial, the United Nations Truce Supervision Organisation earned praise from all quarters.

The hardening of attitudes between the **superpowers** and their allies during the Cold War affected the UN, including its peacekeepers. The Soviet Union, having abandoned its seat on the Security Council just before the US-led Korean mission (see pages 18–21), attacked the UN for being pressured by the United States, which its news agencies branded '**imperialist**'. The member-states which volunteered their troops for this mission were termed 'lackeys' and the military leaders were depicted as aggressive monsters in political cartoons. For their part, American reporters were always quick to find a **communist** motive behind any Soviet support for peacekeeping ventures, as in the Dominican Republic (just south of the United States in the Caribbean Sea) in 1965 and 1966.

Propaganda in the 1950s accused the United States of using nerve gas during the Korean conflict.

Credit and criticism

For the most part, however, most UN peacekeeping missions have been judged on their own terms. The media find the UN presence in conflict-torn areas to contain a high 'human interest' element. To put it bluntly, images of burning houses and refugee convoys sell newspapers and increase television ratings. For the journalists on the scene, however, the risks are as great as those faced by the peacekeepers. In May 2000, two photo-journalists died in action while trying to shed light on the complicated UN Peacekeeping mission in the African state of Sierra Leone.

For their part, UN peacekeepers realize that although some news stories concentrate on these negative elements, having the constant publicity means that their missions are more likely to retain the full support of the participating states. The media in certain countries – such as Canada, Ireland and Finland – treat their own peacekeeping troops as heroes. It was in this spirit, and largely based on favourable reporting in the world press, that the United Nations Peacekeeping Forces were awarded the Nobel Peace Prize in 1988.

Who learns what?

The last decade of the 20th century brought several media-related topics to the forefront. These dealt broadly with the information that the public receives and how the international community acts on it. The first was a basic question of access. Reporters covering the Gulf War in 1991 (see pages 38–41) found that they had limited access to battle areas. Most of the information came from strictly controlled press briefings, conducted in a large part by US military officials. Many in the media saw this approach as deliberate: much of the protest against the US involvement in Vietnam was driven by critical reports by the world's press. The United States, it was argued in 1991, was not going to let such media-led criticism ruin its efforts against Iraq.

Soon after assuming his post in 1992, UN Secretary-General Boutros Boutros-Ghali aimed some criticisms back at the media. He went to great lengths to praise international support for the UN efforts in the former Yugoslavia. But, he wondered out loud, why was it that there was no similar outcry about the crisis in Somalia at the same time. Could it be that war in Europe was more newsworthy than the many conflicts in Africa? As the first African to hold the post of Secretary-General, he was sensitive to the needs of the Somalis, but he had touched on a raw nerve. The world media, as well as reporting the progress of UN peacekeeping missions already under way, can – by its choice of what is important – influence where such missions will be sent.

Senior UN peacekeepers, such as these officers in Sarajevo, have to explain their actions to the world's media.

Counting the cost

There are many costs to consider when we talk about the UN peacekeeping operations. There is, of course, the financial cost, which rises and falls according to the number of operations being carried out. Then there is the cost in terms of reputation if the UN becomes involved in a mission that is considered to be either badly planned, misguided or is judged to be an outright military failure. Most important of all is the cost in terms of human life – the deaths of civilians or of the peacekeepers themselves. But before discussing these costs further, it is worth first looking at the similarly wide range of contributions to the UN peacekeeping effort.

Who contributes?

Since the first UN peacekeeping mission in 1948, some 118 nations have contributed military personnel at different times. And although it is easy to think that major military powers such as the United States, Russia and the UK provide the most troops, many small countries contribute large numbers of personnel. For example, at one point in 1998 Austria, Bangladesh, Finland, Ghana, Ireland, Norway and Poland all had more than 700 troops involved in UN peacekeeping missions. Some countries, such as Canada and the tiny Pacific island nation of Fiji, have taken part in nearly every UN peacekeeping operation.

The number of missions has increased over the years. The UN established 13 operations in the first 40 years of its existence, but since then has launched 36 new missions. At its peak in 1993, the total number of UN peacekeepers – including military and civilian personnel – totalled more than 80,000, from 77 countries.

The price of peacekeeping

Between 1948 and June 2000, 1648 UN personnel lost their lives on peacekeeping missions, although accidents accounted for more deaths than hostile acts. During the 1990s, 211 members of the UN force in the former Yugoslavia died while trying to restore peace to the region.

The cost in reputation

Eighteen UN peacekeeping operations have been undertaken in Africa – more than on any other continent. And although it can look to some successes along the way – helping to resolve disputes in Chad/Libya, Namibia and the Central African Republic – the UN peacekeepers have struggled, or even failed to meet their brief in other African missions.

The ultimate sacrifice

The deaths in May 2000 of peacekeepers in Sierra Leone – the first major peacekeeping operation of the 21st century – underline the ultimate sacrifice that is paid by those who strive to end conflict. Although the toll of lives of UN peacekeepers has been high, their deaths in war have enabled the world to build a peace.

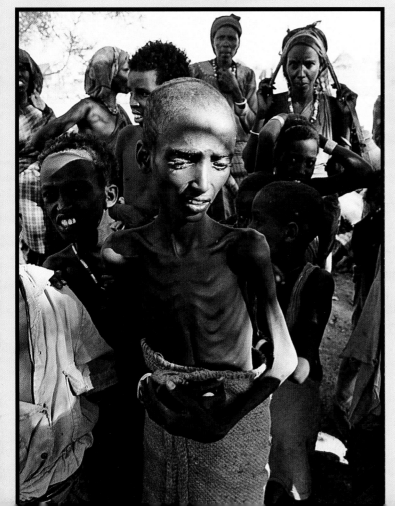

A starving teenager waits for emergency food supplies in Somalia, a 'hot spot' that exposed the limitations of UN peacekeepers.

Somalia seemed to continue its spiral into chaos in 1992 and 1993, despite the presence of UN peacekeepers. And the ethnic conflict in Rwanda entered a brutal phase after UN peacekeepers left the capital, Kigali. Some 400,000 people died in the ensuing bloodbath. These operations were conducted against a terrible backdrop of either famine or **genocide**. Another explanation is that the peacekeeping briefs didn't go far enough, leaving many hundreds of thousands of civilians exposed to bloodshed.

Such failures expose the UN to fierce criticism. Sometimes those who are most critical are from countries that oppose the overall structure of the UN itself. Many in the United States, for example, complain of the UN's wastefulness, and at times the US has been slow to meet its basic contributions to the UN. The UN meets these challenges by pointing out that for every dollar that governments spent on military activities in one year (1997), less than a quarter of a cent (0.25 per cent of spending) went to UN peacekeeping. The US share of the UN Peacekeeping budget that year came to $386 million, or less than $1.45 per US citizen.

Biography – Boutros Boutros-Ghali

Boutros Boutros-Ghali became the UN's first African Secretary-General when he assumed the post in 1992. He was born in Egypt, educated at the Sorbonne in Paris and at Columbia University in New York. This international education enabled him to become fluent in French and English, as well as his native Arabic. He first worked as a law professor and journalist, and then assumed a series of high-ranking positions in the Egyptian government, notably as Minister of State from 1977 to 1991.

While pursuing his career as a diplomat, Boutros-Ghali showed a particular interest in Third World development and the unequal distribution of wealth between rich and poor countries. He helped resolve several African conflicts and to get the release of South African political activist Nelson Mandela from a South African prison in 1990.

Boutros-Ghali succeeded Javier Pérez de Cuéllar of Peru on 1 January 1992 to become the UN's sixth Secretary-General. It was a huge responsibility, since the UN was expected to play an even greater role in settling international disputes because the **Cold War** had just ended. He steered the UN through a difficult period, which included the peacekeeping involvements in the former Yugoslavia as well as major operations in Somalia and Rwanda. And as if to back Boutros-Ghali's views, the UN chose another African – Kofi Annan of Ghana – to succeed him in 1999.

Boutros Boutros-Ghali presided over the United Nations during one of its most turbulent periods – the 1990s.

The future of UN peacekeeping

US President George Bush had described a 'new world order' in the wake of the UN-sponsored victory in the Gulf War (see pages 38–41) in 1991. He was referring to a world in which the former divisions of the **Cold War** had disappeared, leaving countries freer to cherish their independence from **superpowers**. Unfortunately, with that freedom came a new sense of nationalism – sometimes destructive – which set the stage for a series of conflicts around the world.

Within a year of the end of the Cold War, which is usually linked to the break-up of the Soviet Union in 1991, the UN found itself embarked on a greater series of peacekeeping missions than it had seen at any previous time. Several of these missions, including those in Sierra Leone, East Timor and even the former Yugoslavia have continued into the 21st century and few can doubt that there will be more. The UN has looked back on the difficulties it has faced in performing its peacekeeping role and has entered the new millennium with a renewed sense of purpose. It has also begun forming essential partnerships with other international and regional groupings as a way of providing back-up and extra focus to its own efforts.

Australian UN peacekeepers fan out through the countryside of East Timor in an effort to preserve the territory's independence from Indonesia.

French UN peacekeepers disarm civilians during the Kosovo crisis of 1999.

New partnerships

Some of the military alliances that began as Cold War groupings, including **NATO** and the South East Asian Treaty Organization (SEATO) have changed their pattern of operation to take on more of a peacekeeping role. NATO, for example, played an important part in controlling the skies during the Bosnian crisis in the former Yugoslavia (see pages 42–45) and later in the Kosovo crisis in Serbia. In each case NATO worked either directly with the UN peacekeepers or with their support. The UN benefited by having more military clout to back up its efforts, thereby saving costs – and possibly lives – by having such assistance.

Africa has taken a lead in using regional groupings to resolve conflicts. The Organization for African Unity (OAU), with member-states from across the continent, is a respected forum for airing grievances and for providing mediation. Its recognition of Western Sahara (see page 36) in 1983 provided important backing for the UN's subsequent involvement in the disputed area. In 2000 Eritrea turned to the OAU for back-up for a long-standing dispute with its neighbour Ethiopia. On a more regional level, the Economic Community of West African States (ECOWAS) has proved to be a strong force for peace in West Africa.

The Secretary-General's forecast

The UN Secretary-General plays no direct role in setting up individual peacekeeping missions, but his leadership sets the tone for the longer-term strategy of the Security Council, which does initiate such operations. In February 2000, UN Secretary-General Kofi Annan provided a detailed report on UN peacekeeping. In it he addressed many of the problems faced by the UN and outlined potential solutions.

Annan stressed that new missions have increasingly complex **mandates**, which call for increased time and administrative duties, not to mention extra financial costs. He pointed out that the UN is sharing some of these burdens with international and regional organizations (see page 55) as well as with international financial institutions such as the World Bank and the International Monetary Fund. This co-operation also enables a flow of aid to reach affected areas even after the peacekeeping work is done.

Much of the organizational work will be co-ordinated by the Department of Peacekeeping Operations, which will play an important role in monitoring existing operations as well as preparing for new ones. It will also be able to free up UN personnel involved with missions that are winding down, in order to clear the ground for the quick start-ups of any new missions. These measures, along with many other proposals to streamline the core UN operation, offer a chance to achieve the UN's stated aim – of being able to provide a well-organized, disciplined and well-informed peacekeeping force within the minimum time possible.

The UN flag – a symbol of hope and security.

Unexpected benefits

Few would argue that, despite the occasional setbacks in planning and the disputes over funding, UN peacekeeping has had more than its share of successes. Most missions achieve the core aim of providing neutral forces who act as a reason – or even an excuse – for conflicting parties to stop fighting. But there has also been a major contribution in the wider field of international relations – providing a blueprint for peace in the era since the end of the **Cold War**. The signals were there even when the former Soviet Union, poised to unravel within months, approved the US-led intervention in the Gulf War (see pages 38–41). Since then Russia and the United States have been able to use their might to work together for peace. Some old suspicions still linger, despite the fall of the **communist** system, but the common goal of world peace and stability is a force for unity. There is a telling image from 1995, when world leaders sought to secure a lasting peace in war-torn Bosnia. The presidents of Russia (Boris Yeltsin) and the United States (Bill Clinton) were seated side by side in a garden overlooking some unspoilt countryside near New York. No concrete proposals emerged from this particular meeting, but the body language said it all: the leaders of two former enemies were looking ahead with the same vision, seeking grounds for support rather than division.

Major change on the horizon?

In May 2000, UN Secretary-General Kofi Annan stated that several of the guiding principles of UN peacekeeping needed to be rethought. More than 100 UN peacekeepers had been held hostage by rebel forces in Sierra Leone, and the force lacked the firepower and mandate to impose order on rival factions in the country. Annan argued that UN peacekeeping missions should have more weapons and wider powers to enforce a settlement. In addition, there should be times when UN peacekeepers abandon the notion of neutrality. He said that many of today's conflicts were unlike those of the first UN peacekeeping missions, when national leaders could be forced into settlements by international pressure. The more recent conflicts, like that in Sierra Leone, were often sparked by unofficial military leaders who could only be swayed by decisive military action.

Appendix
Completed UN peacekeeping operations

Africa

Angola
January 1989–June 1991
United Nations Angola Verification Mission I (UNAVEM I)
June 1991–February 1995
United Nations Angola Verification Mission II (UNAVEM II)
February 1995–June 1997
United Nations Angola Verification Mission III (UNAVEM III)
July 1997–February 1999
United Nations Observer Mission in Angola (MONUA)

Central African Republic
April 1998–February 2000
United Nations Mission in the Central African Republic (MINURCA)

Chad/Libya
May–June 1994
United Nations Aouzou Strip Observer Group (UNASOG)

Congo
July 1960–June 1964
United Nations Operation in the Congo (ONUC)

Liberia
September 1993–September 1997
United Nations Observer Mission in Liberia (UNOMIL)

Mozambique
December 1992–December 1994
United Nations Operation in Mozambique (ONUMOZ)

Namibia
April 1989–March 1990
United Nations Transitions Assistance Group (UNTAG)

Rwanda
October 1993–March 1996
United Nations Assistance Mission for Rwanda (UNAMIR)

Rwanda/Uganda
June 1993–September 1994
United Nations Observer Mission Uganda–Rwanda (UNOMUR)

Sierra Leone
July 1998–October 1999
United Nations Mission of Observers in Sierra Leone (UNOMSIL)

Somalia
April 1992–March 1993
United Nations Operation in Somalia I (UNOSOM I)
March 1993–March 1995
United Nations Operation in Somalia II (UNOSOM II)

Americas

Central America
November 1989–January 1992
United Nations Observer Group in Central America (ONUCA)

Dominican Republic
May 1965–October 1966
Mission of the Representative of the Secretary-General in the Dominican Republic (DOMREP)

El Salvador
July 1991–April 1995
United Nations Observer Mission in El Salvador (ONUSAL)

Guatemala
January–May 1997
United Nations Verification Mission in Guatemala (MINUGA)

Haiti

September 1993–June 1996
United Nations Mission in Haiti (UNMIH)
July 1996–July 1997
United Nations Support Mission in Haiti (UNSMIH)
August–November 1997
United Nations Transition Mission in Haiti (UNTMIH)
December 1997–March 2000
United Nations Civilian Police Mission in Haiti (MIPONUH)

Asia

Afghanistan/Pakistan
April 1988–March 1990
United Nations Good Offices Mission in Afghanistan and Pakistan (UNGOMAP)

Cambodia
October 1991–March 1992
United Nations Advance Mission in Cambodia (UNAMIC)
March 1992–September 1993
United Nations Transitional Authority in Cambodia (UNTAC)

India/Pakistan
September 1965–March 1966
United Nations India-Pakistan Observation Mission (UNIPOM)

West New Guinea
October 1962–April 1963
United Nations Security Force in West New Guinea (West Irian) (UNSF)

Europe

Croatia
March 1995–January 1996
United Nations Confidence Restoration Organization in Croatia (UNCRO)

January 1996–January 1998
United Nations Transitional Administration for Eastern Slavonia, Baranja and Western Sirmium (UNTAES)
January 1998–October 1998
United Nations Civilian Police Support Group (UNPSG)

Former Yugoslavia
March 1992–December 1995
United Nations Protection Force (UNPROFOR)

Former Yugoslav Republic of Macedonia
March 1995–February 1999
United Nations Preventive Deployment Force (UNPREDEP)

Middle East

Iran/Iraq
August 1988–February 1991
United Nations Iran-Iraq Military Observer Group (UNIIMOG)

Lebanon
June–December 1958
United Nations Observation Group in Lebanon (UNOGIL)

Middle East
November 1956–June 1967
First United Nations Emergency Force (UNEF I)
October 1973–July 1979
Second United Nations Emergency Force (UNEF II)

Yemen
July 1963–September 1964
United Nations Yemen Observation Mission (UNYOM)

Current UN Peacekeeping operations

Africa

Democratic Republic of the Congo
November 1999–
United Nations Organization Mission in the Democratic Republic of the Congo (MONUC)

Sierra Leone
October 1999–
United Nations Mission in Sierra Leone (UNAMSIL)

Western Sahara
April 1991–
United Nations Mission for the Referendum in Western Sahara (MINURSO)

Asia

East Timor
October 1999–
United Nations Transitional Authority in East Timor (UNTAET)

India/Pakistan
January 1949–
United Nations Military Observer Group in India and Pakistan (UNMOGIP)

Tajikistan
December 1994–
United Nations Mission of Observers in Tajikistan (UNMOT)

Europe

Bosnia-Herzegovina
December 1995–
United Nations Mission in Bosnia-Herzegovina (UNMIBH)

Croatia
January 1996–
United Nations Mission of Observers in Prevlaka (UNMOP)

Cyprus
March 1964–
United Nations Peacekeeping Force in Cyprus (UNFICYP)

Georgia
August 1993–
United Nations Observer Mission in Georgia (UNOMIG)

Kosovo
June 1999–
United Nations Interim Administration in Kosovo (UNMIK)

Middle East

Golan Heights
June 1964–
United Nations Disengagement Observer Force (UNDOF)

Iraq/Kuwait
April 1991–
United Nations Iraq-Kuwait Observation Mission (UNIKOM)

Lebanon
March 1978–
United Nations Interim Force in Lebanon (UNIFIL)

Middle East
June 1948–
United Nations Truce Supervisions Organization (UNTSO)

Suggested reading

Organizations that help the world: United Nations, by Michael Pollard – Watford, UK: Exley Publications, 1993

Deliver us from Evil: Peacekeepers, Warlords and a World of Endless Conflict, by William Shawcross – New York, US: Simon & Schuster, 2000

Blue Helmets: The Strategy of UN Military Operations, by John F Hillen – New York, US: Brasseys, 1998

Evolution of UN Peacekeeping: Case Studies and Comparative Analysis, by William J Durch (ed) – New York, US: St. Martins Press, 1993

Useful websites

http: //www.UN.org
The main UN website has many links to pages dealing with its peacekeeping operations. There are full listings of all UN missions along with maps, participating nations and mission briefings.

Other interesting sites include:

http://www.globalpolicy.org
Providing another good overview, this site also examines the underlying strategy behind many of the more prominent UN missions.

http://www.globalpolicy.org/ security/peacekpg/reform
This site, a spin off from the previous site, looks at the future of UN peacekeeping and reform, particularly in the light of the recent report by the UN Secretary-General on the subject.

http://pk.kos.net
This Canadian site shows Canada's national pride in the role its soldiers have played in UN peacekeeping missions, and it includes a number of stories and anecdotes from the soldiers themselves.

http://www.crisisweb.org
The main website of the International Crisis Group, a private multinational organization committed to anticipating, understanding and preventing conflict.

http://www.relief.int
This website provides up-to-date information on humanitarian aid and relief issues and operations around the globe, including much of the UN involvement.

Glossary

Allies the group of countries, including the Soviet Union, UK and US, which joined forces to fight Germany and Japan during the Second World War

amphibious able to operate either on land or water

annex to absorb territory into the borders of a country or city

annihilation complete destruction

antagonism active hostility or opposition

armistice an agreement by both sides in a conflict to stop fighting

artillery the branch of the armed forces specializing in cannons and other heavy weapons

buffer a border between two conflicting nations or regions

ceasefire a suspension of fighting

charter the written set of principles for an organization

coalition a group of countries that join together for a common purpose

Cold War the state of hostility between Soviet powers and Western powers after the Second Word War

colonies areas or countries settled by and under the control of the people of another country

Commonwealth a group of independent countries once ruled by the UK which promote economic and cultural links among themselves

communism, communist a system of rule that calls for government ownership of property and companies

conscription forcing people to join the armed forces

covenant a solemn agreement

decommissioning taking (arms in this case) out of service and dismantling them so they cannot be used

deliberative talking about something in order to reach a decision

democratic a government where the people exercise power by choosing and electing representatives

deposed suddenly and forcefully removed from office

denunciation a statement that condemns someone or something

dictatorship government by one powerful, unelected, and often cruel, leader

embargo stopping trade with a country

entente a friendly understanding or alliance between two or more countries

ethnic cleansing removing people from a different ethnic background from a region, usually by force

expansionist (of a country) intending to widen its borders, possibly through the use of force

free enterprise a system of government opposed to

individuals can own property and companies

genocide the deliberate killing of a very large number of people from a particular nation or ethnic group

guerrilla fighting in small armed bands, as opposed to large armies

imperial having power over an empire

implement put a plan or idea into practice

judicial dealing with matters of justice

legislative having the power to make laws

mandate the detailed set of instructions for a mission

mediator someone who tries to resolve a dispute by talking to both sides

NATO the North Atlantic Treaty Organization, a military group formed to represent the United States and its allies in the Cold War

nationalize to claim ownership of a private company and put it in the hands of the government

nation-states countries with recognized independence

oppressive relentlessly cruel and unfair

partition to divide up a country or region

posthumously occurring after someone's death

propaganda information that is biased or designed to mislead

proxy a representative, who acts on behalf of another person or country

referendum a nationwide vote on an important issue

reparations money paid to one's enemy after being defeated in a war

repressive allowing no freedom of protest

revenue a country's annual income from which public or other expenses are met

sanctions economic measures, such as a stoppage of trade, to persuade a country to change its policies

satellite a country that, although supposedly independent, is really controlled by another country

secession withdrawing formally from a federation or organization

sovereign for a country, having full control of its territory

superpower a country of immense economic, political and military influences; usually refers to the United States and the Soviet Union

unconditionally with no exceptions

veto to vote against something

volatile likely to explode

Warsaw Pact a military alliance of communist countries during the Cold War, aiming to act against the efforts of NATO

Index

2001 title
Oct-29/20
TC-45
Lost Oct-20